FEUER + WEHR

© 1990 Franklin Watts

First published in Great Britain
    1990 by
Franklin Watts
96 Leonard Street
London EC2A 4RH

First published in the USA by
Franklin Watts Inc
387 Park Avenue South
New York
NY 10016

First published in Australia by
Franklin Watts
14 Mars Road
Lane Cove
NSW 2066

UK ISBN: 0 7496 0222 8

Printed in Belgium

Designed by
K and Co

Photographs by
Associated Press
Port Authority of New York and
    New Jersey
Civil Aviation Authority
Rosenbauer
Simon Gloster-Saro
Hong Kong Fire Service
Metropolitan Police
Oskosh
SAS Group
Angloco
FBM Marine
Frank Spooner Pictures/Gamma
Israel Police
N.S. Barrett
Birmingham International Airport/
    Carmichael

Technical Consultants
Heathrow Airport
Civil Aviation Authority

A CIP catalogue record for this
book is available from the British
Library

The Picture World of

Airport Rescue

Norman Barrett

CONTENTS

Franklin Watts

London • New York • Sydney • Toronto

Introduction

Flying is one of the safest means of travel. On average, there are far fewer injuries and deaths from air crashes than there are on the roads.

Safety is of great importance to airports and airlines. They do all they can to prevent accidents or strikes by terrorists. If an accident does occur, airport emergency sevices are always on hand to rescue survivors.

△ An airliner "crashes" on landing at Kennedy International Airport, New York. This is not a real crash, but part of a drill for the airport emergency services.

△ Firemen spray foam on a burning plane in a fire drill.

▽ "Casualties" are attended to during an emergency exercise.

On the scene quickly

Apart from sabotage by terrorists, most air accidents occur at or around airports during take-off or landing.

It is vital for the emergency services to be on the scene quickly — to prevent or put out any fire and to rescue passengers. First on the scene are fire trucks called rapid intervention vehicles

▽ A rapid intervention vehicle must be fast to be able to reach the scene of a crash quickly. This vehicle has a monitor for spraying foam, a fire-fighting platform, and floodlights for operation at night.

△ Firemen wear
special clothing when
getting close to a fire
to protect them from
burning fuel.

▷ Police as well as
firemen help to co-
ordinate rescue
operations.

Fire

Fire is usually the greatest danger when a plane crashes, especially on take-off when the fuel tanks are full. All airports have special fire trucks on hand for this kind of emergency.

Airport fire-fighters are rarely needed. But they go to training schools and have regular fire drills so that they know exactly what to do in an emergency.

△ At fire training schools, firemen can practise fire-fighting techniques on real passenger airliners.

10

△ An aluminium fire fighting suit with a special hood may be worn as protection from flames and smoke.

▷ Airport firemen practise on the various types of fire that may confront them. For example, they might have to tackle a running fuel fire from the wing tanks or a high engine fire from an airliner such as a Tri-Star.

◁ A robot fire-fighting vehicle sprays foam on a burning airliner during a trial. These robot devices are operated by remote control, and may be used when a plane's fuel tanks are in danger of exploding.

Minor airports and airfields that do not need large fire trucks use smaller rapid intervention vehicles.

▷ A Land Rover foam tender carries all the fire-fighting needs of a small airport.

▽ The Pacer is built on a Dodge chassis. It has a driver-controlled foam monitor, ladders and emergency lighting, and carries 1,200 litres (260 gall) of water.

Emergency hospital

ILE EMERGENCY HOSPITAL
EDY INTERNATIONAL AIRPORT
MEDICAL DEPT.

△ A mobile hospital unit is equipped with an operating theatre for on-the-spot surgery.

Emergency hospitals may be set up at some large airports for a major incident. If a jumbo jet crashes or if planes collide on the runway, there may be hundreds of casualties. In such cases, it may be necessary to perform operations on the spot.

Some airports have mobile hospital units that can be driven to the scene of a crash. Hospital tents may be erected quickly in an emergency.

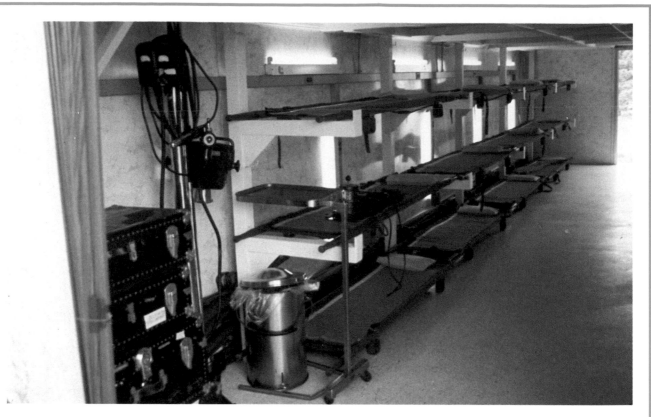

△ Inside an emergency hospital, showing stretcher beds where a large number of casualties may be treated and prepared for surgery.

▽ Inside a hospital tent, where survivors may be comforted and less serious cases may be treated.

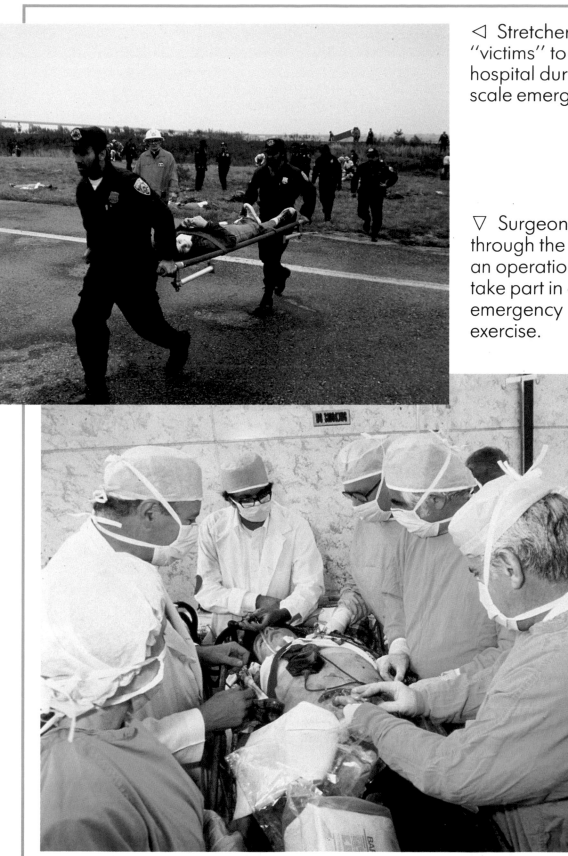

◁ Stretchering "victims" to a mobile hospital during a full-scale emergency drill.

▽ Surgeons go through the motions of an operation as they take part in an emergency hospital exercise.

Off-runway rescue

Some accidents occur when aircraft overshoot the runway on landing or fail to get off the ground when taking off.

The rescue services must be prepared to travel over rough ground or through wooded areas to reach a crashed aircraft. Rescue operations may also take place on water if the airport is near a river or on the coast.

△ The landing strip at Hong Kong's Kai Tak airport juts into the harbour. Both sea and land rescue services were on the scene quickly to save most of the passengers when this airliner overshot the runway in 1988.

▷ The tailplane is recovered from the river after an airliner crashed on take-off at Washington D.C. in 1982.

◁ Rescue boats look for survivors from an airliner that skidded into the East River off the runway at La Guardia Airport, New York, in 1989.

△ An emergency launch, as operated by some coastal airports. It carries fire-fighting monitors as well as rescue apparatus for 250 people.

▽ Rapid intervention fire trucks must be capable of moving through snow or mud. A powerful engine and large "off-road" tyres enable them to travel at speed on or off the runway.

Getting out quickly

Passengers must be removed quickly from a burning or damaged plane. Airliners have emergency exits with chutes so that passengers can slide to the ground safely. A life-jacket is stored under each seat in case the plane lands on water.

One of the biggest dangers is a smoke-filled cabin. Passengers are advised to crawl to the exits as smoke tends to rise off the floor.

△ Officials and rescue workers study a burnt-out airliner after an accident at Manchester Airport in 1985. An engine had exploded as the plane raced along the runway. Fire and fumes spread quickly through the cabin, killing many passengers. Since then, airlines have taken fresh steps to prevent the rapid spread of fire.

The terrorist threat

Airports and airlines take special security precautions against the threat of terrorists. These are groups of people who, for one reason or another, attempt to hijack or sabotage airliners.

All international airports operate strict security to prevent armed passengers boarding an aircraft and stop explosives being smuggled on in luggage. In some countries, special rescue squads go into action if there is a hijack.

▽ A hooded terrorist in the cockpit of a hijacked airliner in Beirut in 1985. This incident led to the murder of an American citizen, although the rest of the hostages were eventually released.

◁ Armed Israeli police stand guard outside an airliner as a precaution against terrorist attack.

▽ Troops and police in a tank take part in a security exercise outside London's Heathrow Airport after terrorist attacks at Rome and Vienna airports in 1985.

Facts

In-flight emergency
Passengers are sometimes taken ill or injured during a flight. In serious cases, the plane might divert to the nearest airport. Otherwise, the cabin staff are trained to give first aid, and doctors or nurses among the passengers might also help. The crew might radio the airport to be prepared to provide medical help on arrival.

△ An ambulance is ready at the airport to take a sick passenger to hospital.

A small risk
Some people are afraid of flying. Yet the chance of an accident is very small – about one in every half million flights. Major air accidents throughout the world average only about 20 a year. There is a much higher chance of being involved in a serious accident driving to and from the airport!

△ Tackling an aircraft fire at a fire service training school.

Fire training
Airport firemen are highly trained to tackle fires in aircraft and at airports. At their training schools, real aircraft are set on fire to give them practice in "real life" situations. They learn to deal with burning fuel, leaking from either aircraft or airport fuel tankers. They practise rescuing people and learn how to find their way through fire and smoke inside a burning aircraft cabin.

Passenger safety

Cabin crew are specially trained to look after the safety of passengers in an emergency. They learn how to get people out of the plane quickly – through emergency exits and down chutes. They are trained to help people who are ill or hurt. They learn how to use breathing equipment and fight fires.

New measures being developed to improve passenger safety include smoke hoods to help people breathe in a smoke-filled cabin, water mist systems for automatically putting out cabin fires, and fire-resistant materials for seats.

Skyjacking

The hijacking of airliners, also called "skyjacking", is an activity that became a serious threat to passenger safety in the late 1960s. Groups of terrorists began to hijack planes, taking the passengers hostage and threatening to blow up the aircraft or kill the hostages unless their demands were met.

In the United States alone, there were 40 skyjack attempts in 1969, and in 1970 there were 90 skyjacks worldwide. Most skyjacks have been resolved without loss of life. But some have resulted in the deaths of passengers and terrorists or the destruction of the aircraft. New laws and strict security checks have reduced the number of skyjacks since the 1970s.

△ The modern airfield crash tender is designed to respond quickly to any emergency. It carries its own pumps, hoses, rescue ladders, breathing apparatus, portable extinguishers and lighting. It holds 10,000 litres (2,200 gall) of water and 1,100 litres (250 gall) of foam, yet can accelerate to 80 km/h (50 mph) in just 25 seconds.

27

Glossary

Airline
A company that provides regular air transport for the public on fixed routes between airports.

Foam
A lather used for smothering fires. Foam is used especially on burning fuel, where water by itself would only spread the flames.

Hijack
The illegal capture of any vehicle, train or aircraft. Plane hijackers, also called skyjackers, usually force the pilot to fly to a place of their choosing. Most skyjacking is done by terrorists, but there have also been cases of people hijacking a plane to escape from a country.

Jumbo jet
The Boeing 747, the biggest kind of airliner in service.

Monitor
Apparatus fixed to some fire tenders for spraying foam at high pressure.

Rapid intervention vehicle
A fire tender with the equipment necessary for responding quickly to an emergency on or around the airfield.

Sabotage
Any action intended to cause damage or destruction.

Security
The precautions taken at airports and by airlines to ensure the safety of passengers and planes, especially against terrorist activities.

Skyjack
See *Hijack*.

Smoke hood
A hood that passengers can wear over their faces to protect them from smoke if there is a fire in the cabin.

Terrorist
A member of a group organized to cause fear, usually for political purposes.

Index

PRINTED IN BELGIUM BY
proost
INTERNATIONAL BOOK PRODUCTION